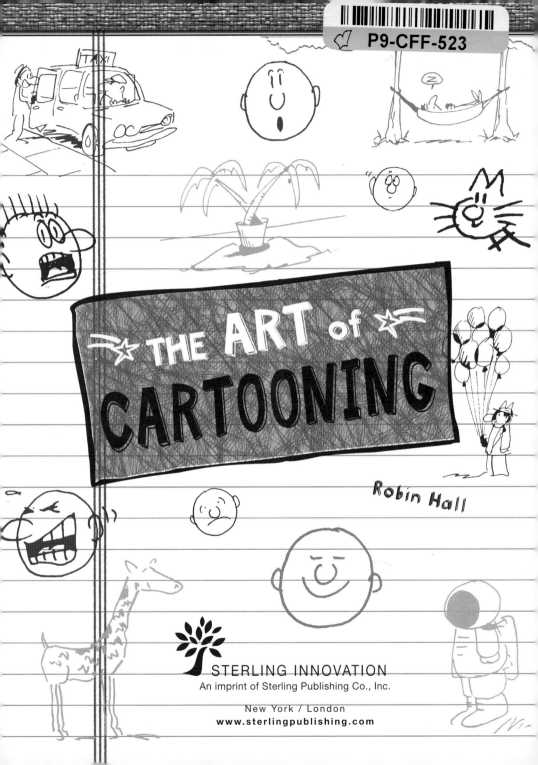

THE ART of CARTOONING

Robin Hall

STERLING INNOVATION
An imprint of Sterling Publishing Co., Inc.

New York / London
www.sterlingpublishing.com

Acknowledgments

Many thanks to: my brother and partner in crime Peter Hall, whose brilliant cartoons have always inspired me; my brother Michael Hall for making the book comprehensible and committing it to disk; Pat McGhee, Gary Hamilton, and Ronnie Baird for their help and encouragement; Maggie Dun, Jon Kimble, Jim Russell, and everyone at Knight Features for helping me on my way; Anne Watts, my favorite editor; and Niki McPherson—I'd be lost without you.

2 4 6 8 10 9 7 5 3 1

Published in 2009 by Sterling Publishing Co., Inc.
387 Park Avenue South, New York, NY 10016

Excerpted from *The Cartoonist's Workbook*
© 1995 Robin Hall
Material originally published in Great Britain by A&C Black (Publishers) Limited

Distributed in Canada by Sterling Publishing
c/o Canadian Manda Group, 165 Dufferin Street
Toronto, Ontario, Canada M6K 3H6
Distributed in Australia by Capricorn Link (Australia) Pty. Ltd.
P.O. Box 704, Windsor, NSW 2756, Australia

Sterling ISBN 978-1-4027-6371-7

For information about custom editions, special sales, premium and corporate purchases, please contact Sterling Special Sales Department at 800-805-5489 or specialsales@sterlingpublishing.com.

CONTENTS

Preface

CARTOONING ALWAYS APPEALED to me because I assumed that most cartoonists didn't have to get up early in the morning. Well, that's not the full story: I was also fascinated by the way that cartoons were able to encapsulate all aspects of human life—from the serious to the humorous, the earth-shattering to the mundane—in one frozen image.

However, I wasn't one of those lucky people born with bundles of creative ability. In fact, I couldn't draw a cartoon to save my life; even my stick figures looked unshapely. If I was to get into cartooning I knew that I'd have to do some serious work. So I studied every cartoon I could lay my hands on, hundreds of them, and I practiced and practiced . . . and practiced.

As my work improved, I began to realize that, if I followed certain guidelines and shortcuts when creating a cartoon, satisfactory results were almost guaranteed. Gradually, I developed these guidelines and shortcuts into a method which finally opened the door for me into the cartooning world.

This book is my attempt to share this method with all those who, like myself, are full of enthusiasm but short on natural ability. For beginners and professionals alike, I have added a wealth of reference material which I hope will be of lasting value. I wish all you budding cartoonists good luck, and if you make it, it's true, you WON'T have to get up so early in the morning!

Robin Hall

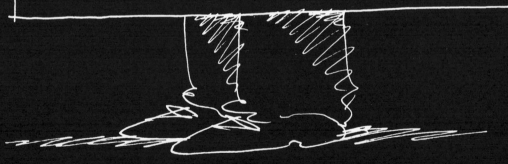

CHAPTER ONE

DRAWING CARTOONS
AS EASY AS ABC

Drawing Cartoons

The process of drawing cartoons can be likened to that of writing (or "drawing") the alphabet. You don't need a special talent, just some useful guidelines and a **LOT** of practice.

For instance, when you learned the alphabet, you were probably told that to make an "A" you had to join two lines together in a point, "like a church steeple," and then connect these lines with another one drawn horizontally.

In other words, you had to "draw"

And then came the important bit—you were made to REPEAT this hundreds of times until you could do it with ease.

1 Now, with cartooning, it is the same type of process, only with new guidelines. For instance, to draw a face, I could tell you to begin by drawing a "C", flattened a bit, like a sausage:

2 Next, add 2 dots just above the right-hand corner:

3 Then draw a line down from the middle of the flattened "C":

4 Now draw a "reverse C" opposite the flattened one:

5 Then draw some angled lines above the right-hand dot:

6 Finally, draw a line for a mouth—and you've drawn a face!

Now comes the important part—PRACTICE this!

Keyhole Ken-The Cartoon Character

Now let's use the same process to draw a basic human cartoon figure which we can later expand upon.

Begin with a keyhole shape by drawing a circle with a "box" shape under it (the sides of which "move in" toward the top).

 Then This is a keyhole shape

Draw it lots of times until it looks like the one above.

Now we can add features to this using the guidelines.

FLAT "C"	2 DOTS	REVERSE "C"	ANGLED LINES	MOUTH	"L" SHAPED ARM	3 LEG LINES	2 FEET AND HAND

Now comes the important part—repeat it again and again. Use lined paper and keep all the drawings the same size. This is an important thing to learn.

Continue to practice drawing "Keyhole Ken" until you FEEL that he looks BALANCED. It could take some time.

UNBALANCED   **BALANCED**

Keyhole Ken's Tall Friend Len

After you have practiced drawing Keyhole Ken facing in one direction, draw him facing the other way.

REMEMBER—PRACTICE, PRACTICE, PRACTICE.

So instead
of this

draw him
this way

Now, to make things more interesting we can begin to draw people of different heights. For instance, say you wanted to draw a tall friend beside Ken, first draw Ken then begin his friend higher up.

Start Len's
head higher up

Now remember, if a person is tall, EVERYTHING must be taller so obviously the following can't work:

This needs to be extended
down to the ground

extended

Now practice this over and over again on lined paper.

How to Draw Keyhole Ken From All Angles

Cartoon characters must be able to face and look in **ALL** directions. There are three basic body poses that will allow the head to look **ANYWHERE**. You already know two of the body poses—facing left and facing right. The third one is facing **TOWARDS** us.

First draw the keyhole shape:

Now, as before, you need to add a nose, eyes, ears, hair, mouth, arms, legs, and feet. First of all, just LOOK at the "keyhole" and IMAGINE where these features would be if Ken were facing towards you. Then go through the usual process, but draw each feature where you imagine it should be.

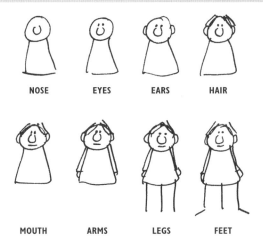

NOSE	EYES	EARS	HAIR

MOUTH	ARMS	LEGS	FEET

REMEMBER—these are the same features turned around to face TOWARD us.

Before beginning the face, you can make Ken look in ANY direction you want by "pointing" his nose in that direction.

Now go through the process of building up the face by using the nose to help you picture where the eyes, ears, hair, and mouth are to be drawn.

Some Poses

Arms

RELAXED   **"OH YEAH!"**   **"SORRY"**   **"WHAT!"**   **"DON'T KNOW"**

"UH-OH!"   **"MMM . . ."**   **"AAARGH!"**   **"NOW LET ME SEE"**   **"OVER THERE"**

Legs

RELAXED   **WALKING**   **RUNNING**   **SKIDDING**

SITTING   **KICKING**   **SITTING**   **LEANING**

Full Body

FALLEN DOWN   **RUNNING**   **ON ALL FOURS**

REMEMBER—PRACTICE, PRACTICE, PRACTICE.

Keyhole Costumes

Let's see how we can draw **ANY COSTUME** using the keyhole shape as a guide.

Ken already has a "coat" shape, so to begin with, you could change this to various coats and tops using the keyhole shape to help you IMAGINE the item you desire.

| SUIT JACKET | DUFFEL COAT | RAINCOAT | CARDIGAN | ARMY JACKET | JUMPER | T-SHIRT | BLOUSE |

Then apply this IMAGINING process to trousers and skirts.

| CUFFS | JEANS | FLARES | BAGGIES | SHORTS | SKIRT | DRESS |

Then there are hats . . .

| TRILBY | UNIFORM CAP | TWEED CAP | BOWLER | SAILOR'S HAT | HARD HAT | CROWN |

. . . and shoes:

| BOOTS | SNEAKERS | FOOTBALL CLEATS | HIGH HEELS | SLIPPERS | GALOSHES |

REMEMBER—PRACTICE, PRACTICE, PRACTICE.

Some Additional Features

Remember, practice these facing the other way as well.

Glasses

| PLAIN | SHADES | READING | STYLISH | GOGGLES | MASK |

Beards

| PLAIN | SHIPWRECKED | SANTA | UNSHAVEN | MUSTACHE | JUST SHAVED |

Hair

Men

| STRAIGHT | CURLY | YOUTHFUL | UNTIDY | NEAT | BALD |

Women (smaller noses)

| WAVY | STRAIGHT | STYLED | BEHIND EARS | PERMED | BUN |

ACCESSORIES

| WALKING STICK | UMBRELLA | SHOPPING BAG | KNAPSACK | BABY CARRIAGE |

A Collection of Keyhole Characters to Practice

First, draw lots of keyhole shapes; then, while looking at the keyhole, imagine ("picture") the costume you want and draw in the more obvious features.

Through the Ages

Babies

LARGE HEAD, ROUNDED BODY, CAN'T STAND UP

SMALL NOSE, BIG EYES, BIG EARS, NOT MUCH HAIR

Children

SCRUFFY HAIR, SMALL BODY, SMALL NOSE, BIG EARS, T-SHIRT, SHORTS, SNEAKERS

YOUNG HAIRSTYLE, VERY NEAT, SMALL NOSE, CUTE CLOTHES, SENSIBLE SHOES

Teenagers

QUITE TALL, FASHIONABLE, REBELLIOUS

Thirty-Something

TIDIER, MORE CONSERVATIVE, PRACTICAL, "SENSIBLE" CLOTHES, STYLISH

Middle-Aged

COMFORTABLE CLOTHING, HEAVIER BUILD, SHORTER, WEARY LOOK, SLIGHTLY RUFFLED, MORE HUNCHED OVER

Elderly

ANY OLD CLOTHES, SHORTER AGAIN, THINNER, VERY HUNCHED OVER, FACE "SQUASHED", FALSE TEETH?

Expressions

PLAIN TALK   **AMUSING**   **FUNNY**   **HYSTERICAL**   **OBSTINATE**   **INSINCERE**

ANGRY   **VERY ANGRY**   **ANNOYED**   **DEPRESSED**   **DISTASTEFUL**   **GUILTY**

SLEEPY   **SAD**   **HAPPY**   **SMUG**   **DAZED**   **HUNGOVER**

SURPRISED   **SHOCKED**   **HORRIFIED**   **SCARED**   **EMBARRASSED**   **CALM**

RELIEVED   **PARANOID**   **LISTENING**   **CURIOUS**   **EXASPERATED**   **"HERE WE GO"**

BORED   **HUNGRY**   **CONFIDENT**   **CONCENTRATING**   **WATCHFUL**   **SULKING**

Keyhole Ken-Man of Many Disguises

Now that you can draw Ken in many poses and with various expressions, you can begin to change him into any character you wish.

Let's begin with the face. Each feature on Ken's face can be altered to depict a certain type of person.

Ken's basic face shape is this:

Now each of the features can be altered in turn.

Noses

Eyes

Chins

Hair

Mouths

Now to build a character, IMAGINE each feature. Say, for instance, you wanted to draw a sly villain with a pointed nose, "slit" eyes, no chin, slicked-back hair, and a tense physique.
Make your way through the process of building a face using the type of features you've imagined.

POINTY NOSE

"SLIT" EYES

NO CHIN

SLICKED HAIR

"TENSE" SHOULDERS

Study other cartoon characters to see how features are built up and practice copying them.

Developing Complete Keyhole Characters

Let's say you want to draw two cowboys—a "good guy" and a "bad guy" who are competing for the attentions of a rancher's daughter, Emmy-Lou. First **IMAGINE** how they **MIGHT** look in a typical Western.
Good guy—tall, strong chin, well built, confident, dressed in white
Bad guy—short, no chin, stooped over, sneaky eyes, dressed in black
Emmy-Lou—medium height, hair in a ponytail, flowery dress
Now, start by drawing the good guy's **BASIC** keyhole shape (with legs).

NOW WE CAN CALL THIS HEIGHT TALL.

THE BAD GUY IS SHORT, SO HIS HEAD IS LOWER.

THE GIRL IS MEDIUM, SO HER HEAD IS IN BETWEEN AND SHE'LL BE THINNER.

Drawn close together we have:

ROUGHLY ADD COWBOY GEAR AND A DRESS FOR EMMY-LOU.

Now add basic expressions.

EXAGGERATE CERTAIN FEATURES

CHEST OUT   BACK TENSED UP

ARM ON HIP —CONFIDENT

DRESS

When you practice all this, be quick and loose. Don't worry if it looks scribbly, you can easily tidy it up by tracing it.

How to Turn Keyhole Characters into Finished Cartoons

You now have three keyhole characters which look very sketchy.

One way to draw a "finished" cartoon from the keyhole sketch is to trace over it and only draw in IMPORTANT lines.

For example, the good guy's head would be traced by going through the process for building a face so that only IMPORTANT lines are drawn. Use tracing paper, or thin white paper if you can see through it.

SKETCH   TRACING PAPER   NOSE   EYES   CHIN   EAR   HAT   ETC . . .

Also, when tracing you can exaggerate certain features.

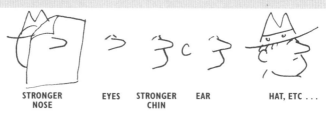

STRONGER NOSE   EYES   STRONGER CHIN   EAR   HAT, ETC . . .

If you continue this process with the three characters, you could end up (after a lot of practice) with this:

Special Effects-Shadows

There are plenty of books that cover this subject in detail so rather than repeat it all, I'll just go over a few simple "tricks" that can be used to good effect.

GROUND SHADOWS

A simple shadow can give a character a greater sense of being GROUNDED, rather than floating in "whiteness."

MAKE IT DARKER ON ONE SIDE OF THE OBJECT
AND KEEP IT LOOSE AND SCRIBBLED.

FLOATING   **GROUNDED**

These shadows can also indicate WHERE a character is in relation to the ground.

UNCLEAR   **ON TOES**   **OFF THE GROUND**   **UNCLEAR**   **OFF THE GROUND**

They can also give objects in midair more solidity and "height."

OBJECT SHADOWS

The simple rule to follow is to shade an object on the side farthest away from the light source (YOU pick the light source—it's your cartoon).

FOR EXAMPLE

Special Effects-Movement Lines

When objects move, we see a "sweeping" image, not just one image. Check this out by waving your hand around.

Sweep Lines

In a cartoon, we show this "sweeping" movement by drawing lines in the DIRECTION of the movement ("sweep lines").

Object Lines

But also, to make it clear what these lines indicate, we need to add a few more lines to represent the OBJECT at various points along its line of travel.

The curved lines represent
the object at previous stages

If an object is waving about in ALL directions, we can add just a few object lines to indicate this.

The general rule is—if you want to indicate small movement then just draw in some OBJECT LINES in the places the object has moved through. If you want to indicate a larger sweeping movement then draw in SWEEP LINES to indicate direction AND some OBJECT LINES (usually close to the object) to indicate that the object is moving.

SMALL MOVEMENT OBJECT LINES

SWEEP LINES AND OBJECT LINES HELP TO MAKE THIS MOVEMENT CLEARER

Keyhole Crowd

A good thing to practice is crowd scenes to force you to think about different heights, expressions, poses, clothing, etc. Although it's actually quite easy, the finished product is often impressive looking.

First, think HEADS and draw some (not all) of them at different heights. IMAGINE the heads within a crowd and QUICKLY draw them in relation to where you think the ground might be.

GROUND LEVEL

Now draw in keyhole bodies and JUST THE OUTER LINES of the legs. Don't add feet yet.

NO INNER LEG LINES YET

Now give them all a direction to face in. Use the NOSES to point the way. Now you can draw in the extra leg line as well (and feet).

Finally, simply keep building up costumes, expressions, and whatever else comes to mind. Don't OVERDO it. People don't really dress THAT differently.

Keyhole Animals

The rules that we have applied to cartoon people can also be applied to cartoon animals. Let's begin with the face.

Human

| NOSE | EYES | CHIN | EAR | HAIR | ETC. |

Dog

Cat

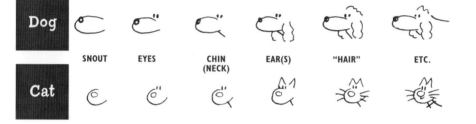

| SNOUT | EYES | CHIN (NECK) | EAR(S) | "HAIR" | ETC. |

Now see if you can use this process to draw the following assortment of animal faces.

| BIRD | COW | MOUSE | ALLIGATOR |

For animal bodies we can still use the keyhole technique but more often than not we will want to keep it in mind rather than draw it out. The thing to remember is that animals have similar shapes to human beings but everything is bent over as if we were touching the ground with our hands.

WE COULD USE THIS IMAGE TO DRAW A "KEY-HOLE" CAT.

Animal Essentials

The one thing most beginners forget about with cartoon animals is to draw in their NECKS.

Most beginners draw this:

 BUT ALL ANIMALS HAVE LONGISH NECKS.

After the neck is in place then we draw in the back and legs. Quick cartoon legs can simply be like very thin human legs (and add on a "thigh" to the back legs).

FACE   **NECK**   **BACK**   **LEGS (AND THIGH)**

You can see this process in many animals. Try to draw them.

Use the keyhole technique if you want a quick idea of an image you have in mind. Change it to suit each animal. Use it as a reference sketch. Picture in your mind the most BASIC shape of the animal you wish to draw and sketch it out QUICKLY. Then use this as a guide for a more detailed drawing.

   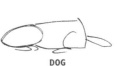

COW   **CAT**   **DOG**

Raining Cats and Dogs

Here are some typical poses and some essential features for our most popular cartoon animals. Remember—always practice drawing things in the other direction as well.

FEET

UPRIGHT

LONG WHISKERS   SHORT WHISKERS   LONG HAIRED

THIN   FAT

ADVANCED DRAWING
TECHNIQUES

Drawing Without Picture Reference

The ultimate goal in cartooning is to be able to draw any image that comes into your head without having to spend three hours looking through half a dozen encyclopedias for reference.

To do this you first have to learn to **VISUALIZE** an image in mind. You have to play detective. Analyze the object: see it in sections, shapes, and sizes. Imagine you are actually looking at the object, as if you could touch it. Try to bring the image in your mind more into focus.

After you have done this you can use any or all of the following techniques to get your image down on paper.

1. Break the image down to basic shapes.

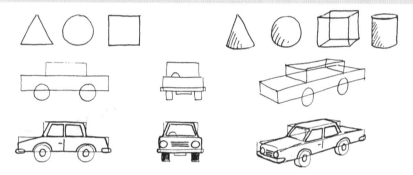

2. Draw a "framework" to use as guidelines.

3. Build outward from one section of the object.
Build in the same way you build up Keyhole Ken. If you do this quickly, it can give a nice, loose effect.

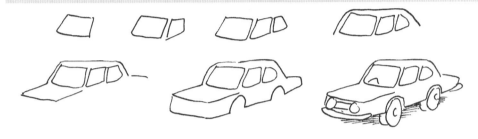

4. Draw the image as a child might draw it.

5. Try and "see" the object on the paper, then sketch it in.

Can you "SEE" a shark here, chasing the fish?

6. Keep doodling.
Make an attempt at the image, then keep tracing over it and change various parts until it takes the shape you want. Be loose and quick to begin with. Very often the first doodle will be the best one.

7. Draw the outline first, then fill in the rest.

8. Only use a part of the object or find an easier angle.

9. Be extremely loose and sketchy.

10. Draw important points of reference first.

11. Be your own model for difficult poses.
For instance, if you wanted to draw someone kicking a ball, stand up, pose yourself in the position, and then take each part of your body a step at a time. Check the angle of your upper body—then DRAW IT. Pose again in the same position, check the angle of one of your legs—then DRAW IT. Pose again, and so on . . .

BACK ANGLED   LEG BENT, FOOT CENTERED   OTHER LEG BENT, THIGH HORIZONTAL   LEFT ARM ANGLED DOWN AND BENT   ETC.

12. Use a mirror for difficult expressions or hand positions.

13. Get someone else to pose and do a quick sketch.

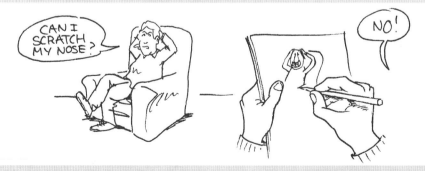

14. If you run into difficulties, make a snack!

Developing a Personal Style

It is helpful to develop a unique style but don't make uniqueness your chief concern. Aim to please yourself. If you can draw characters that YOU find funny or intriguing, then you will find it easier to come up with gags. Look at other cartoon styles that you enjoy and figure out what you most like about them. Copy to begin with, but keep experimenting. Mix styles up, exaggerate, be ridiculous! Use the Keyhole Ken process to draw an infinite variety of characters.

Personal Style-Line and Shading

THIN LINE

THICK LINE

LOOSE (TRY HOLD-ING YOUR PEN HALFWAY UP)

TIGHT

SKETCHY (NEEDS TO LOOK STYLISH RATHER THAN UNFINISHED)

MINIMALIST

ANGULAR

"LOOSE" ANGULAR

ROUNDED

CHILDLIKE

FLEXIBLE NIB

SOFT PENCIL

SCRIBBLED

SKETCHY

LIGHT

CROSS-HATCHED

ETCHED LOOK

HIGH CONTRAST

STIPPLED

CRAYON

ACTUAL DESIGNS

MECHANICAL TINT

SCRIBBLED CRAYON

TIGHT DETAILED

Composition

While there are no right or wrong ways to arrange the various elements of a cartoon, there are certain guidelines that beginners can utilize to make their drawings more effective and more interesting.

Let's use the following setup to consider the guidelines.

KEN

A HOUSE

A TREE

BACKGROUND

1. Is there a mood you wish to express?

This may determine how you lay out the various elements. Think like a film director.

IS THE HOUSE A THREATENING PLACE?

OR A WELCOMING PLACE?

IS KEN NERVOUS?

IS IT FAR AWAY?

2. Balance (i)

Do the elements in your scene fit together on the page or in the panel in an interesting and pleasing way?

TOO STRAIGHTFOR-WARD

A BIT CRAMPED

TOO MUCH BLANK SPACE

THIS IS MORE INTERESTING

SEEK FOR THIS BALANCE IN ALL YOUR LAYOUTS

Balance (ii)

Keep important elements grouped together rather than scattered but
don't overdo it. Try and link the elements in some way.

| TOO SCATTERED | TOO TIGHT | MORE BALANCE |

3. The Center of Attention

To make your drawings more interesting or to direct the reader's attention,
EMPHASIZE the more important details of your scene in some way.

WHEN ALL THE ELEMENTS HAVE THE SAME DETAIL THERE IS NO CENTER OF INTEREST

IN THIS DRAWING KEN STANDS OUT MORE

THE IMPORTANT ELEMENT DOESN'T HAVE TO BE CENTRAL

4. Depth

There are various ways to create a sense of depth.

OVERLAPPING   **"DISTANCE" PERSPECTIVE**   **"ANGULAR" PERSPECTIVE**   **SHADING**   **LINE CONTRAST**

5. Setting the Scene

Learn to "set the scene" with a minimum number of objects.

6. Balance of Light and Dark

If you use areas of black or shading remember they are
an important part of the composition.

| TOO OBVIOUS | MORE INTERESTING | TOO LITTLE | TOO MUCH | MORE BALANCE |

7. Variation

Aim for variation in your strip cartoons or comic pages but don't
overdo it. Having several panels exactly the same could be part of your
"variation." When you rough out a strip or page always consider how
the panels work TOGETHER as ONE picture.

BIT BORING

VARIATION IN CHARACTER SIZE OR PANEL SIZES

VARIATION IN PERSPECTIVE

VARIATION IN BLACK OR WHITE AREAS

VARIATION IN POSES OR EXPRESSIONS

VARIATION IN PANEL BORDERS

**KEEP IN MIND THAT REPETITIVE PANELS CAN ALSO BE
A USEFUL WAY OF CONVEYING FEELINGS OF BOREDOM, TENSION, ETC.**

8. Use the Borders

**THIS INCLUDES
US—THE VIEWER** **BREAKING OUT** **THESE
LINES
BORDER
THIS
DRAWING** **EXTREME
CLOSE-UP** **VERY FAR AWAY**

Exaggeration

Most amateur cartoonists have had some form of art training, which has probably conditioned them to draw what they "see" rather than what they "feel" and so their cartoons often have a lifeless quality. Good cartoons have movement, they "speak" for themselves. If a character is in a rage, smoke comes out of his ears. A character "in love" literally "floats on air." Don't be shy. Exaggerate, try to animate your characters, even try and bring your characters' SURROUNDINGS to life.

Perspective-Five Useful Rules

The farther away an object gets, the smaller it is.

The closer an object gets, the bigger it appears.

FARTHER AWAY

3. Horizontal lines ABOVE your eye level will APPEAR to move DOWNWARD as they get farther away from you.

FROM ABOVE

FROM GROUND LEVEL

4. Horizontal lines BELOW your eye level will APPEAR to move UPWARD as they get farther away from you.

HORIZONTAL LINES ABOVE HORIZON MOVE DOWNWARD AS THEY GET FARTHER AWAY

EYE LEVEL
IMAGINED HORIZON

HORIZONTAL LINES BELOW HORIZON MOVE UPWARD AS THEY GET FARTHER AWAY

5. Any horizontal lines that are PARALLEL to each other (running in the same direction) will converge at a point on the horizon called the vanishing point (VP).

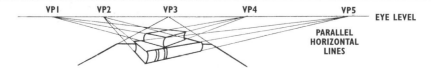

VP1   VP2   VP3   VP4   VP5   EYE LEVEL

PARALLEL HORIZONTAL LINES

Perspective by Instinct

Perspective rules are often best applied after an attempt has been made to place objects instinctively, because very often a cartoon drawing can lose vitality if it is worked out too perfectly in the sense of perspective.

For instance, should you want to draw someone standing in a room with lots of pictures on the walls, don't make perspective your sole concern. Think about the composition first. Is there a particular mood you wish to convey? Are the pictures overpowering? Is the room big or small? Where are we viewing the scene from? Are we low down or high up? Do some quick sketches and try to get them roughly in perspective.

| CLOSE UP | FAR AWAY | FROM BELOW | FROM BEHIND |

You may find that you are perfectly happy with one of these roughs, but should you wish to be more accurate with the perspective, draw in some "perspective lines" OVER your rough and then correct parts of the original rough, though trying not to lose the vitality of the sketch.

SAY YOU PICK THE VIEW FROM BELOW . . .

IMAGINE WHERE THE HORIZON LINE IS.

NOW EXTEND ONE LINE THAT LOOKS CORRECT TO THE HORIZON.

USE THAT POINT TO DRAW IN OTHER LINES THAT ARE PARALLEL.

NOW USE THESE LINES TO CORRECT THE ROUGH PERSPECTIVE.

FINALLY, TRACE A CLEAN IMAGE USING A LIGHT BOX.

A More Realistic Keyhole Ken

KEN IS ABOUT 4 HEAD HEIGHTS TALL.

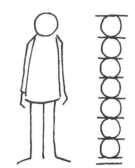

THE AVERAGE PERSON IS ROUGHLY
7 1/2 HEAD HEIGHTS TALL.

FOR A CARTOON 5 HEAD HEIGHTS ARE BEST.

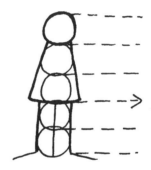

THIS MAKES THE BASIC KEYHOLE
SHAPE EASY TO WORK OUT.

AS WELL AS BEING TALLER, THE AVERAGE
PERSON IS USUALLY THINNER THAN KEN.

OBVIOUSLY, REALISTIC FACES WILL MAKE A
BIG DIFFERENCE (SEE PAGE 44).

SHOULDERS WILL ALSO ADD TO THE REALISM . . .

EVEN A NECK . . .

X ✓

HANDS WILL
NEED TO BE
DRAWN MORE
REALISTICALLY.

MAKE THE CLOTHING MORE DETAILED
. . . AND THE BODY PARTS MORE FLEXIBLE.

Caricatures

To tackle caricatures you first need to learn how to construct a slightly more realistic "basic" face so that you can exaggerate your subject's more prominent features. Use Keyhole Ken as a guide.

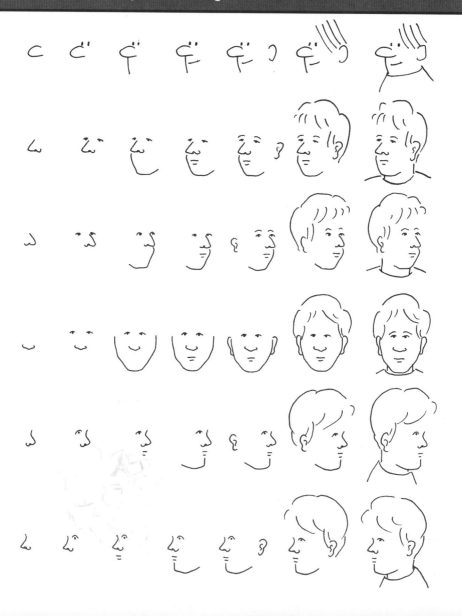

By varying the features of these basic face shapes you can come up with some pretty interesting characters. Experiment with added details, such as fuller lips and eyes, double chins, wrinkles, hairstyles, etc.

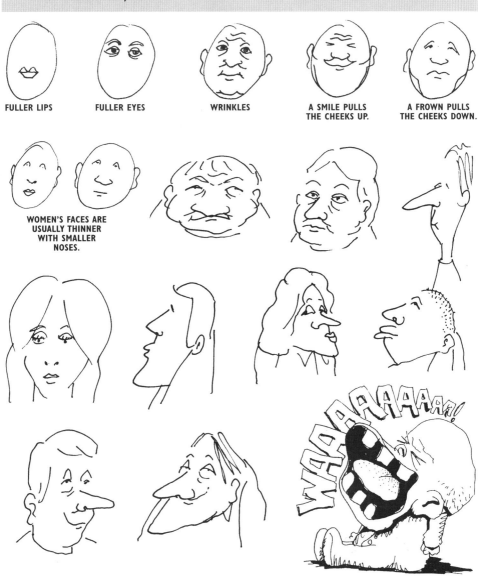

FULLER LIPS

FULLER EYES

WRINKLES

A SMILE PULLS THE CHEEKS UP.

A FROWN PULLS THE CHEEKS DOWN.

WOMEN'S FACES ARE USUALLY THINNER WITH SMALLER NOSES.

Now let's use this process to draw caricatures of two very distinctive personalities, Laurel and Hardy. If you are working from a photograph, make a photocopy of it measuring about 3 inches square. Now trace around the main outlines—but don't attempt any shading.

As you build up the caricatures exaggerate the more prominent features.

AVERAGE NOSE   EYES HIGH UP   LONG FACE   POINTED EARS   MOUTH NEAR NOSE, DISTINCTIVE GRIN, CHEEK LINES   UNTIDY HAIR

WIDER NOSE   SLIT EYES   ROUNDED FACE   "MORE USUAL" CLOSED MOUTH   VERY DISTINCTIVE HAIR

CLOSE TO THE TRACING   EXTREME EXAGGERATION

Basic Anatomy

Should you wish to draw very realistic cartoons it is helpful to build up the various parts of the body using more workable underlying shapes. Then you can use this framework to draw your final image.

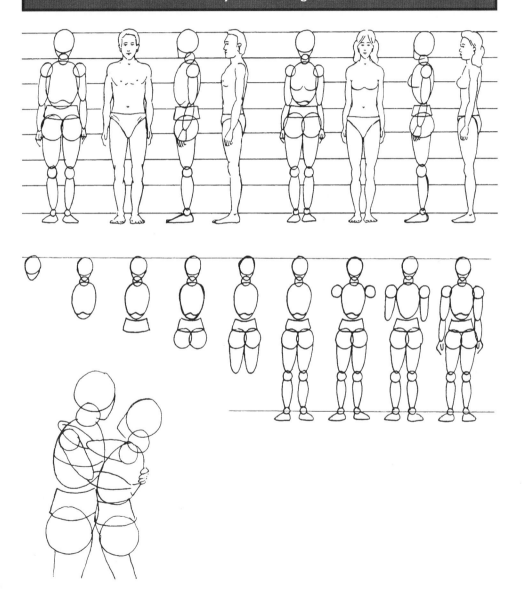

REMEMBER—PEOPLE COME
IN ALL SHAPES AND SIZES.

USE A STICK FIGURE OR KEYHOLE
FIGURE TO GET A ROUGH POSE.

THEN BUILD UP
THE CORRECT
BODY SHAPES.

THEN TRACE A
FINAL IMAGE.

Basic Anatomy-Heads, Hands, Feet

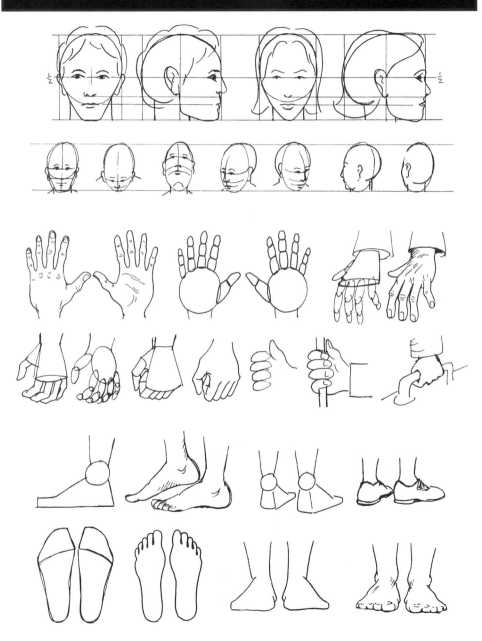

Useful Poses

Useful Poses 2

Useful Poses 3

Useful Poses 4

Cartoon Language

Cartoon Language 2

Texture and Form

SOFT

SHARP

THE PULL OF A BUTTON

METALLIC

FINE

WOOLLY

COARSE

HAIRY

SPONGE

BROKEN

BONE

WAX

REFLECTIVE

SMOKE

CREASED

STRINGY

STEAM

SACK

HOT

OLD

NEW

SOILED

Texture and Form 2

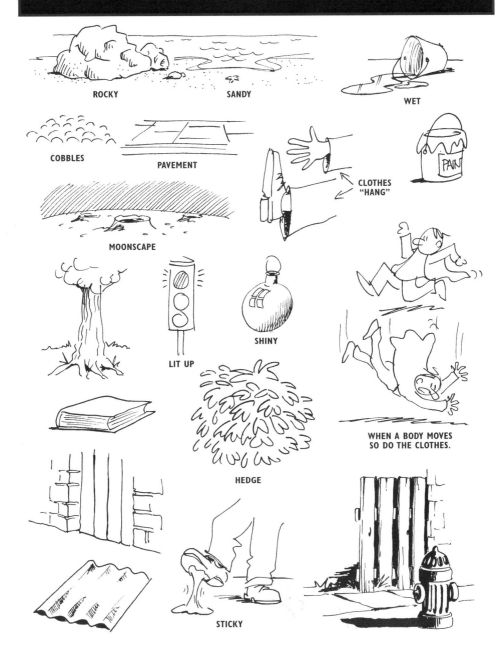

ROCKY

SANDY

WET

COBBLES

PAVEMENT

CLOTHES "HANG"

PAINT

MOONSCAPE

LIT UP

SHINY

WHEN A BODY MOVES SO DO THE CLOTHES.

HEDGE

STICKY

Useful Indoor References

Useful Outdoor References

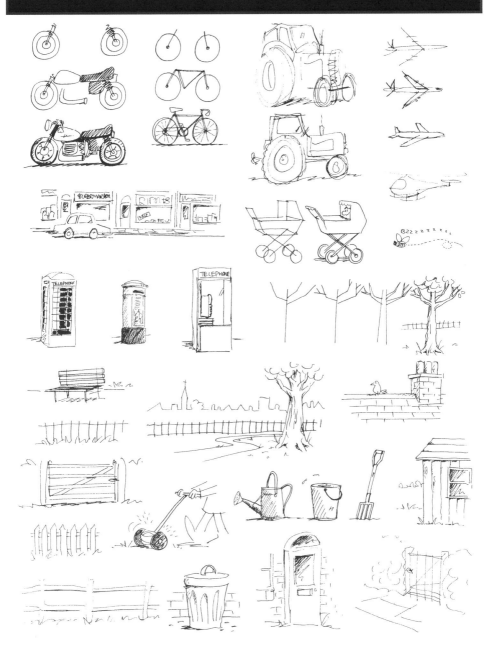

Shading

COME FLY WITH ME – LET'S TAKE OFF TO PERU....

THE SCARE-CRAW
Or some one wraith clad in disguise

OWOOOOOOOOOOOOOOOOooo...

Coloring Your Work

While there are numerous ways to color your cartoons, there is one GUARANTEED way to make your coloring look professional, and that is by using PANTONE* markers.

A lot of cartoons nowadays are computer-colored and markers can give you a similar effect—clean, flat colors (which don't buckle the paper). Figuring out which ones to use is a process of trial and error. Study other cartoonists' work and decide upon a minimum number of colors that will get you started. But be prepared for a shock when you find out how much they cost!

However, when it comes to coloring body parts, skin-colored markers are not always effective, and I would recommend you use colored pencils instead.

The process is simple. Apply the markers to good-quality photocopies of your black and white drawings. Should the black lines bleed under the color, try another copying machine. Initially use these photocopies to experiment with until you find color combinations which feel harmonious and look professional. You can use your final version as finished artwork. Once you get the feel for it you soon find that markers are easy to use and enable you to get through a lot of coloring reasonably quickly.

Here are a few shades that I recommend.

*The TRIA™ range of PANTONE®
(Pantone, Inc.'s check-standard trademark
for color) by Letraset® Color Markers

WARM GRAY 1T	
WARM GRAY 3T	very useful as "color shading"
COOL GRAY 1T	
COOL GRAY 3T	
480 - T	- a good brown for trees, fences, furniture, clothes
292 - T	- a "blue jeans" color
375 - T	- grass green
277 - T	- a light blue sky (the lightest there is, unfortunately)
679 - T	- a pastel purple color for clothes, settees, beds, etc.
134 - T	- a sandy yellow color

The Light Box

Draw something on a page, and place a clean white sheet of paper on top. You may just barely see the drawing on the bottom page. Now, keeping the pages together, hold them up to a light and you'll see that the image becomes much clearer and could easily be traced (if it weren't so awkward).

This is how a light box works. It is really just a tracing machine. You can simply place a clean sheet of paper over your quick sketches on the box, turn on the light, and trace a more finished, corrected drawing. You can even move the two pages around to better position various elements in your drawings. It is a very useful piece of equipment.

Lettering

There is no standard style of lettering for cartoons. Anything goes, even untidy writing could look effective as the "voice" of an untidy character. If, to begin with, you just want to make your lettering look more professional, here are a few tips.

Practice writing the alphabet again and again on lined paper. Keep experimenting with the structure of the letters and the spacing.

STRUCTURE   SPACING

The letter "S" can be difficult to master. The secret is to make the upper curve SLIGHTLY smaller than the lower one.

8 8 8

SSSSSSSSSSSSS

Keep practicing until you come up with an alphabet that looks confidently written, evenly balanced, and generally pleasing to the eye.

ABCDEFGHIJKLMNOPQRSTUVWXYZ

Try out as many drawing instruments as you can for lettering. You'll only find out through trial and error which are best suited to your abilities and needs. An easy way to place lettering in your cartoon strips is to use a light box. First of all rough out the strip the same size as the finished artwork will be, and try to place the lettering instinctively. From this you can then trace a more accurate "rough," which can then be used in turn to help you draw the finished strip.

TRY THE LETTER IN ONE OR TWO "ROUGHS."   **TIDY IT UP AND CENTER IT BY TRACING IT ON A LIGHT BOX.**   **USE GUIDELINES IF YOU NEED TO.**   **YOU DON'T HAVE TO "CENTER" EACH LINE.**

We read dialogue from left to right or top to bottom.

CONTOURED

SPEAKER OUT OF SIGHT

PAUSE

PAUSE

QUESTION — ANSWER

CONTINUE

MY DOG'S GOT NO NOSE

AWFUL!

HOW DOES IT SMELL?

THE CURSE

HOW TO DO WHITE ON BLACK...

BUGHOUSE

BZIT

ELECTRIC SHOCK

WHACK

Belch.

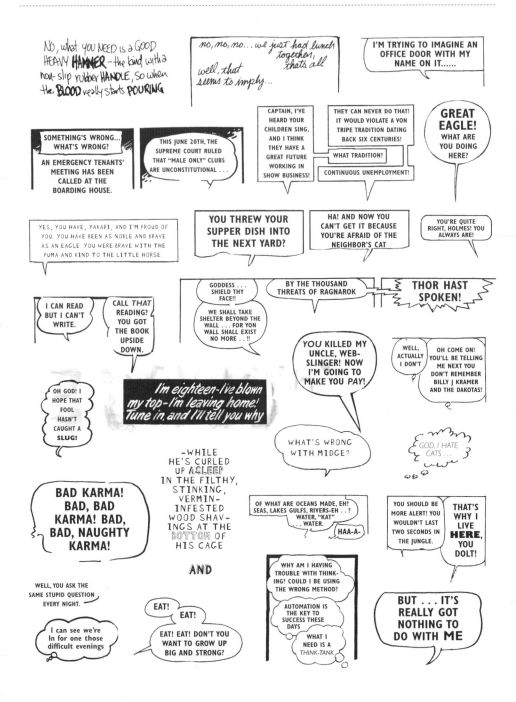

CHAPTER THREE

WRITING GAGS

Writing Gags-Oiling the Machinery

Many people would lead you to believe that the ability to write jokes for cartoons is something you either have or don't have and there's nothing you can do about it. That's **NONSENSE!** You can learn it like everyone else. It's not easy, but it gets easier the more you practice.

It is obviously best to learn how to draw cartoon characters first, but while you are doing so, there are certain things you can do to prepare yourself for writing jokes. Now and then try to be visually humorous with your drawing practice. Just doodle. Take things to extremes.

Start drawing cartoons for friends and family—on letters or notes, or make your own birthday and Christmas cards. Just draw out actual humorous situations you and people around you have been involved in and maybe add a comment or two. Once you start this, people begin to expect it of you, which forces you to think of more and more ideas. This is an easy introduction to writing gags and people love receiving personal cards like this.

POSTCARDS

LETTERS

Try and add humorous captions to illustrations or photos in encyclopedias and magazines.

FOR EXAMPLE:

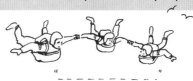

Read as many cartoon books as you can.

Finding a "Gag" Situation

In Cartoonsville, a "one-shot" cartoon is called a "gag."

The first thing you need to find for a gag is a **SITUATION**. The best source of possible situations is an encyclopedia, preferably one with plenty of illustrations. Just flip through it until something catches your eye and then make a **QUICK** sketch of whatever it is.

SPACEMEN CAVEMEN NELSON

Or you can use typical cartoon situations. Don't hesitate to do this to begin with, but later on try and come up with more original setups.

SNAKE CHARMER FLYING CARPET

Don't discard a possible situation that you come across in a magazine or book just because you can't immediately come up with a great joke for it. Sketch it. Der are veys to make ze situation talk!

Let's use the oldest situation in the book to take you through the gag-writing process step by step—the "desert island" scenario. Keep in mind that this process must be studied over a long period of time. Rome wasn't built in a day.

Writing Gags-Step 1: Related Images

The first thing you have to do is make a **START**. Things will not begin to move if you simply sit and stare at your chosen setup. If you **EXPAND** on the situation and draw some related images then you obviously have more to work with. Here are some suggestions—see what you can add to this list.

- What obvious images can you associate with the situation?
- What OBJECTS could possibly be in the scene?
- What CHARACTERS could possibly be in the scene?
- Imagine you are there. Look around, what ELSE do you see?
- Does the scene remind you of anything?
- Try the scene from far away / close up.
- Try the scene from above or below, what could be above or below?
- Change PARTS of the scene—make them different shapes, sizes, textures; make them bigger, smaller, TOO big, TOO small.
- Add more people, less people, too many people, too few people.
- Change the sex of the characters.
- Change their nationalities.
- Try different age groups—elderly, babies, teenagers.
- Change the setting to daytime, nighttime.
- What effect would the seasons have—spring, summer, autumn, winter?
- Place a TOTALLY unlikely object in the scene.
- Is there some BIG event you could imagine taking place?
- Is there some minor event that could spark a situation?
- What is the biggest OBJECT that could enter the scene?
- What is the smallest OBJECT that could enter the scene?
- _____
- _____
- _____
- _____
- _____
- _____
- _____
- _____
- _____

Now try a few of the above suggestions on some of the NEW images you've drawn. You should have plenty.

Example Sketches

Writing Gags–Step 2:
Wider Observations

• What is the TOTAL exaggeration of the situation?
• What would your favorite cartoonists do with the scene?
• Begin a conversation between the characters—anything at all. See where it leads you.
• Set the scene in the past or the future—from BC to 2020.
• Is there a well-known saying or expression about the situation you could incorporate or adapt?
• What feature of the character(s) could be relevant?
• Totally change the props in the scene—be ridiculous.
• Relate the characters' USUAL situation to something else.
• What else could the characters possess, something that might seem unimportant,
  but which might spark off a situation?
• Show the character—as a child / at home / on the toilet / in the supermarket /
  at a movie / restaurant / dentist, etc.
• Imagine different scenarios—why, for example, would people be fleeing for their lives in the scene?
• Why would the police or fire brigade be there?
• Is it an historical event?
• What would a complete twit say?
• Does ANY object in the scene bring to mind ANYTHING else at all that could lead
  to further images?
• What would a child say to his or her parent about the scene—or vice versa?
• Could it be relevant to modern society or the environment, or be a comment on
  politics, advertising, war, capitalism, poverty?
• What would be REALLY sick (though tone this down to something acceptable)?
• What could these people have to say—a child, a tourist, a crowd of onlookers, a police detective,
  an alien, an animal, a TV reporter, a neighbor, a mother, father, pet, husband, wife?

Could any of these characteristics spark off an idea?

Laughing, mad, crying, bored, hungry, nervous, terrified, sad, dead, rich, poor, scruffy, tidy,
bigoted, stupid, envious, in agony, sleepy, insomniac, bad-tempered, passionate, brave,
scared, drunk, in love, sarcastic, embarrassed, henpecked, annoying, overtalkative, smelly,
clumsy, walking disaster, brokenhearted, sulking, fashionable, very weird, hypercritical,
boastful, argumentative, excited, impatient, hysterical, fussy, nosy, fanatical, dictatorial,
artistic, musical, scientific, lonely, reclusive, famous, infamous, pathetic . . .

Example Sketches

Writing Gags-Step 3: "Problem" Method

Cartoons can hold a mirror up to life and very often they can remind us that it's possible to laugh at some of our problems and thereby work through them. Or we can laugh at the man on the desert island because perhaps WE feel isolated sometimes and it's nice to have some company. Maybe we just laugh because we're glad someone is worse off than ourselves.

Gags are often based on the fact that some "problem" exists. Not necessarily serious problems, just some reason why what was meant to happen can't or didn't happen.

It helps to look at your images and ask yourself

- What is MEANT to happen—what could PREVENT this?
- Why do the characters not get along with each other?
- What drama could occur to spark off a humorous situation?
- What could go wrong with the events?
- Could some PART of the scene cause a "problem"?
- Imagine you are one of the characters—whom would you LEAST want to be with or meet in this situation?

THROWS 'MESSAGE IN A BOTTLE' WHICH IS SUPPOSED TO REACH CIVILIZATION—WHAT PREVENTS THIS?

REACHES THE ISLAND. CAN'T GET ON—WHY NOT?

THEY DON'T GET ALONG WITH EACH OTHER. WHY?

APART FROM BEING A CASTAWAY, WHAT ELSE CAN GO WRONG?

Writing Gags—Experimental Doodling

Just draw anything that comes to mind.

Example Sketches

SENDS FOR A BOAT

CHRISTMAS ISLAND?

COCONUTS

BEEN HERE LONG?

Writing Gags-Complete Method

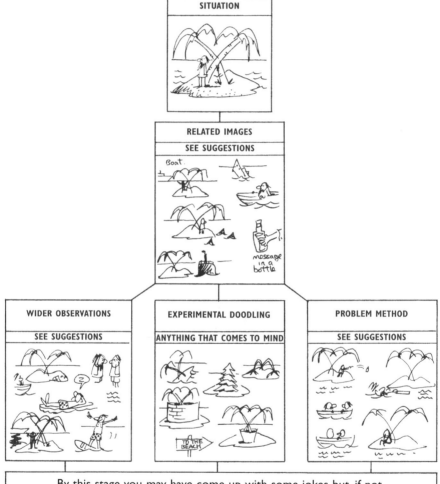

By this stage you may have come up with some jokes but, if not, keep looking, keep experimenting. Be quick, just do loose sketches. If a drawing seems to have possibilities expand on it again using the three methods. The whole point is to set your mind flowing in the right direction so that something amusing will pop into it.

Gag Situations

Cartoon Strips—Where to Begin

Cartoon strips differ from "one-shot" gags in two fundamental ways. First, instead of having the humorous situation confined to a single drawing, you can develop across a series of frames, with the "punch line" appearing in the final one. Second, the characters who appear in the strip are normally the same ones brought together in subsequent strips—indeed, for as long as the cartoonist can keep creating humorous situations for them. This repetitiveness allows the development of the characters' personalities in a way not possible in gags.

The first consideration in creating a workable cartoon strip is to figure out a location or "setup" and then gather up a suitable cast of characters.

You could drive yourself mad by trying to be too original to begin with because everything seems to have been done. If you have a great idea for a cat or a dog, don't scrap it just because of Garfield and Snoopy. It's a big world, and there's plenty of room for more funny cartoon cats and dogs.

Endeavor to be as original as you can but try and let it happen—don't force it. Start drawing characters that appeal to you and see where it leads. The important thing is to get started. After a while you'll begin to understand how it all works and then you'll get ideas for more original setups.

A lot of beginners worry about the size that they should draw a cartoon strip. The best thing to do is to draw the characters at whatever size is most comfortable for you and then use this as a guide to working out your panel measurements. A lot will also depend on what type of drawing instrument you use. There are no fixed rules. Keep experimenting until you feel happy with your artwork.

At the very beginning, don't worry too much about panel sizes or about the pens and paper you should use. All that does is give you an excuse not to work on the important stuff—the drawing and the jokes. Just DRAW, DRAW, DRAW. And STUDY the joke-making process. In finding a location or setup and a cast of characters it is helpful (if you don't go for a "family" strip) to look through encyclopedias, which have tons of images that might help spark something.

Remember, don't give up if the world's most original idea doesn't hit you in the face. Just draw away—experiment—try ANY set of characters (from just a few to a whole town if you wish!) to see how it works. Treat all this as necessary practice. We can learn much from our mistakes.

The next page gives you an idea of the "complete" process you can go through to create a cartoon strip. It is much like the process used for gags with some other things you have to take into consideration. The pages following go into it all in more detail.

Cartoon Strips—The Complete Process

If finding jokes is hard work but you think your setup has possibilities then just keep at the drawing practice. Study the "joke methods" and try them now and then. Be patient, it will all "click" one day. Don't force it, take it slowly.

SETUP LOCATION CHARACTERS ETC . . .

DRAWING PRACTICE

STANDARD POSES

EXPRESSIONS MANNERISMS

AT WORK, REST, AND PLAY

MISCELLANEOUS SITUATIONS
SHOPPING
DRIVING
ON THE PHONE
SITTING, THINKING
FIXING THINGS
DECORATING
VISITING
ETC.

EXPERIMENTAL DOODLING

COLLECTION OF REUSABLE SITUATIONS

THE GAG-WRITING PROCESS

RELATED IMAGES

SEE SUGGESTIONS

WIDER OBSERVATIONS

SEE SUGGESTIONS

"PROBLEM" METHOD

SEE SUGGESTIONS

"THAT'S LIFE" SITUATIONS
MISSING THE BUS
SLEEPING IN
SPILLING YOUR TEA
LOSING YOUR KEYS
FORGETTING YOUR NAME
ETC . . .

OPENING FRAME METHOD

LISTEN TO THE CHARACTERS

Cartoon Strips-Drawing Practice

Standard Poses

If you have a fair idea for a cast of characters, then start to practice drawing them over and over again so that they always look like the SAME characters. This is VITALLY important for a cartoon strip and gets you started without wondering what to do!

Expressions and Mannerisms

When you get to know a set of characters by repeatedly drawing them, it is very useful to let THEM carry out humorous conversations while you kind of "listen in" and write them down. I know that sounds daft but it does happen. By changing the expressions and mannerisms, you can "overhear" new conversations whenever you want.

"I'VE GOT IT!"   **"NAG, NAG, NAG."**   **"OH, PLEASE GOD."**   **"THAT'S A LAUGH."**

At Work, Rest, and Play

The cartoon strips that work best are usually the ones that hold up a mirror to modern society and deal with things we are all familiar with, namely the things we do at work, rest, and play. Draw these situations regularly and use personal experiences.

Miscellaneous Situations

There are a million and one things you might miss when you think generally in terms of work, rest, and play. Things that are still familiar to all of us: shopping, catching the bus, driving, at the vet's, sitting thinking, fixing things, decorating, visiting people, etc. Make up your own list and draw scenes from some of them.

Experimental Doodling

Very often, just drawing your characters in funny poses or in certain settings or costumes or whatever, can help you "see" a joke. If nothing else is working, just doodle—experiment—be loose and exaggerate a lot. Put your characters in unlikely poses and see what happens.

Collection of Reusable Situations

The more you practice drawing your characters, the more you will see certain situations that can be used again and again to get jokes. It's a good idea to collect these into one folder so that you can go through it from time to time. These situations can be handy if your brain dries up.

Cartoon Strips—
The Gag-Writing Process

RELATED IMAGES (see the suggestions on page 68)

This is basically the same process as for "one-shot" GAGS but this time you need to keep the related images within the bounds of your setup.

WIDER OBSERVATIONS (see the suggestions on page 70)

Again, you cannot stray too far away from your setup but do experiment. Always be open to changes and new directions.

The list of expressions on page 16 can be very useful in a cartoon strip.
For instance you might decide to have one of your characters crying—so WHY is he crying, WHAT problem has occurred to make him cry? Etc., etc. This helps your mind begin to work. Always sketch ideas—no matter how daft they may seem at first. The sketch may help you see a really clever idea.

"PROBLEM" METHOD (see page 72)

The best way to understand how this method works is to study other cartoon strips and work "backward" to see how the theme was developed. Then ask yourself how the strip COULD have started off using your idea of a "problem." These problems don't have to be major or serious, just humorous alterations of what was meant to happen in the normal run of events.
For instance, asking yourself "WHY can't character 'A' get out of bed?" is more helpful than just staring at a drawing of that character lying in bed. The aim is to expand on every situation to start your creativity flowing.

"THAT'S LIFE" SITUATIONS (personal experiences)

You know the ones: the missing keys, oversleeping, missing the bus, forgetting someone's name, "putting your foot in it," spilling your carefully prepared snack all over the floor, finally finding a need for something you threw out yesterday, etc. There are a million scenarios with humorous potential right under your nose.

OPENING FRAME METHOD

As mentioned before, sometimes we need to give our mind a kick start before a joke will pop into it. This opening frame method is often very useful for this. Simply mark out two to four panels and draw ANY situation involving your characters in the first panel and then see if any ideas come to mind regarding the complete strip. You could also make your character say something—ANYTHING at all—and see what happens from that. Experiment, draw out lots of three or four panel strips and draw something in each opening panel.

LISTEN TO THE CHARACTERS

Your characters will take on a life of their own once you get a few jokes under your belt. This will give you a direction to go in. The characters will come to life more, and more jokes will follow and so it will build up and become easier. But it takes time, so be patient. I doubt if anyone has created a successful cartoon strip overnight.

Whatever happens, don't ever take it all too seriously or it will show in your cartoons. Work hard, but if it's becoming a chore, stop for a while—wait until you feel in the mood again. If you try to force it you could waste more time in the long run. Our minds still work on things even when we are not consciously thinking about them. Let this natural process take place. Relax and have fun.

Cartoon Strips from Start to Finish

After you have a character or set of characters and have gotten to know them better by drawing them a lot while imagining their personalities, here's one way you could tackle an actual strip.

Pick a Situation

I draw a character called Conrad who sleeps all day. Let's say I was going to work an idea out for him. I might first of all draw him in his favorite place—bed.

Expand on the Situation

From this drawing I would then find as many related images as possible, as I suggested before. For instance, what objects are in the room? There is a clock, a bed, a window, bedclothes, etc. Think of a situation for each item. Does the clock go off? Why would this shock him? Why would it be a problem? Is the bed uncomfortable? Is he thinking about how much he loves the bed? What is outside the window? A window cleaner? A bird chirping? Noisy workmen? How do these things affect him? Do his bedclothes have a cartoon design on them? Is he cold or warm? What else can happen to him because he is in bed? Does someone call? Does he have to get up? WOULD he get up? What is he thinking about? Is he dreaming or having a nightmare? Is there a big spider hanging down from the ceiling?

Quickly draw lots of related images and then expand on each situation again if you need to. Always keep in mind your characters' personalities. How would they react to certain things? Are they sarcastic, lazy, scared, silly . . . ? LOOK at your drawings and LISTEN to your characters as if they were acting out their roles in the world you have set them in. Don't forget to draw various expressions to bring them to life.

Do a Quick Sketch of Your Joke

By going through this "related images" process, I came up with an idea for a strip where Conrad gets really annoyed about noisy workmen outside in the street. I then sketched the basic idea very quickly.

Do a More Finished Rough

Usually these quick sketches have nice spontaneous elements that are worth keeping. Also, from them you can tell if certain panels need to be made bigger or smaller, because of the scene or the amount of dialogue. After taking all this into consideration you could try a few more quick rough sketches and then draw up a more finished rough, the same size as the final artwork will be. When doing this, fit the dialogue in first and build the drawings around that.

Complete the Final Artwork

Your final artwork can now be drawn onto artboard, using your "finished rough" as a guide. Or you could trace a finished drawing from your rough onto paper, using a light box. If you make any mistakes, don't do the whole strip again, just draw the correction on another piece of paper, cut it out, and paste it in.

Little Town Blues

By HALL

More Gag Situations

STREET ARTIST

ON THE STREET

STATUE

TELEPHONE

I SPEAK YOUR WEIGHT

BUS STOP

MEN AT WORK

QUEUE HERE

SALE

GOSSIPS

BACK OF CROWD

MAIL

FLAGS

NEWS

TRAMP

THE END IS

Gag Situations 2

MECHANIC

ROAD SIGNS

PLAYGROUND

MEN AT WORK

SEE-SAW

PUB

BINOCULARS

WASHROOM

BUS/PLANE/CINEMA

WAITER!

Gag Situations 3

DECORATING

HOME MOVIES

BIRD TABLE

I'M LEAVING YOU, THELMA

IRONING

PLAYPEN

CLOTHESLINE

SLEEPWALKER

BEDTIME STORY

MAN IN WARDROBE

WOKEN UP

Gag Situations 4

ABSTRACTIONS

ELEVATOR

ESCALATORS

HIGH-RISE WORKERS

"HOPKINS . . ."

CONVEYOR BELT

"MISS WILSON . . ."

HIGH-RISE

COURTROOM JURY

FUNERALS

Gag Situations 5

"ELEMENTARY, MY DEAR WATSON"

LITTLE RED RIDING HOOD

ROBINSON CRUSOE

GENIE

ZORRO

JACK AND THE BEANSTALK

ROBIN HOOD

DR. FRANKENSTEIN

ANGRY MOB

HUMPTY DUMPTY

MUMMY

RIP VAN WINKLE

ARCHAEOLOGISTS

SUPERMAN

PIED PIPER

GRAVEYARD

HELL

GHOSTS

COUNT DRACULA

DEATH

Gag Situations 6

FIRING SQUAD

ROAD SWEEPER

MONK

SHEEP SHEARER

FIREMEN

FORTUNE TELLER

MUSEUM STATUES

POTTER'S WHEEL

CLIMBERS

ROCK BAND

SCULPTOR

AWARDS

MASSIVE CROWD

PRESS CONFERENCE

THEATRICAL AGENT

Gag Situations 7

THE GODS

WISE MAN

PONDERING THE UNIVERSE

MOUSE

COMPUTERS

CLASSROOM

FILMS

"BREATHE IN"

WEDDINGS

MOVIE SET

MATERNITY VIEWING ROOM

THE MOVIES

CONVENTIONS

Gag Situations 8

TRAFFIC JAM

OVER-PACKED CAR

BILLBOARDS

TOUR BUS

ECHO VALLEY

WELCOME TO

CUSTOMS

LOVERS LEAP

NUDIST CAMP

IGLOO

SUBMARINE

"I NAME THIS SHIP . . ."

SHIPWRECKED

Gag Situations 9

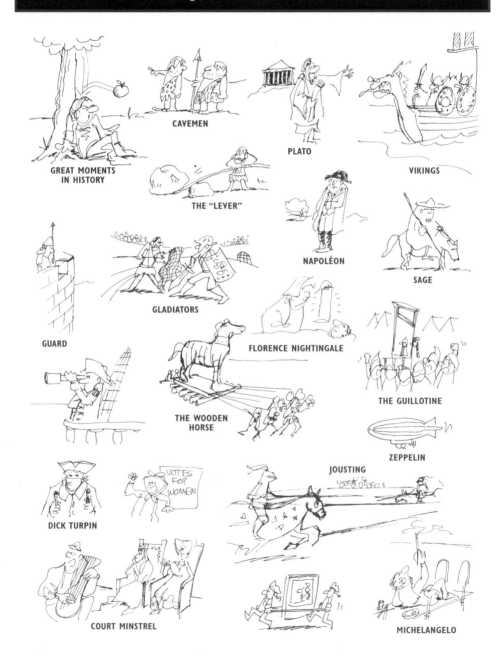

GREAT MOMENTS IN HISTORY

CAVEMEN

PLATO

VIKINGS

THE "LEVER"

NAPOLÉON

SAGE

GUARD

GLADIATORS

FLORENCE NIGHTINGALE

THE GUILLOTINE

THE WOODEN HORSE

ZEPPELIN

DICK TURPIN

JOUSTING

COURT MINSTREL

MICHELANGELO

Gag Situations 10

PEACE PIPE

THE LONE RANGER AND TONTO

DAVY CROCKETT

SHERIFF

COWBOY'S CAMPFIRE

RAIN DANCE

SIESTA

HUNTER

STICK-UP

RODEO

POLICE

PRISON VISIT

GOOD COP—BAD COP

POLICE LINEUP

HARD LABOR

Gag Situations 11

TRICK CYCLIST

SKYDIVERS

JUGGLING

DARTS

THE BEAM

SACK RACE

JOGGING

POLE VAULTER

RELAY RACE

HURDLES

JURY

SKATER

TUG-OF-WAR

Gag Situations 12

OSTRICH

BEWARE
OF THE
BULL

ANT HILL

Index